A Country Without Names

Also by Martin Anderson

Poetry

The Kneeling Room *
The Ash Circle *
Heard Lanes
Dried Flowers
Swamp Fever
The Stillness of Gardens
Black Confetti
Belonging *
Snow. Selected Poems 1981–2011 *
Interlocutors of Paradise
The Lower Reaches *
Obsequy for Lost Things *
Ice Stylus *
In the Empire of Chimeras *

Prose

The Hoplite Journals (complete in one volume) *

The Hoplite Journals I-XXIX *
The Hoplite Journals XXX-LIX *
The Hoplite Journals LX-LXXIX *

An asterisk denotes a Shearsman title.

Martin Anderson

*A Country
Without Names*

Shearsman Books

First published in the United Kingdom in 2022 by
Shearsman Books
P O Box 4239
Swindon
SN3 9FN

Shearsman Books Ltd Registered Office
30–31 St. James Place, Mangotsfield, Bristol BS16 9JB
(this address not for correspondence)

www.shearsman.com

ISBN 978-1-84861-795-7

Copyright © Martin Anderson, 2022.
The right of Martin Anderson to be identified as the author of this work has been asserted by him in accordance with the Copyrights, Designs and Patents Act of 1988.
All rights reserved.

ACKNOWLEDGMENTS

Under Jui-yi Shan previously appeared in slightly altered form in *Shearsman* magazine, Winter 2017/18. *Road to the North* appeared in the Winter 2018/19 issue also in slightly altered form, and *Flowering Midnight* in the Spring/Summer issue of 2020.

Cover image: Luftwaffe photograph of the September 1940 bombing of Thames-haven oil refineries. The inlet of Hole Haven (bottom left of the photograph) on Fobbing Marsh in the Lower Hope region of the Thames, where the *Nellie* in Joseph Conrad's *Heart of Darkness* was moored close to the Chapman lighthouse, is obscured by thick smoke; but not the rest of the creek meandering, in a north north easterly direction, towards the foot of Fobbing village.

Contents

Rock Star Celebrates Birthday
at Exclusive Country House Retreat / 9

Road to the North / 10

Alder / 20

Driven Dust / 27

Where No Snow Falls / 28

Reliquary / 36

Uncomfortably at Home / 66

Road of Dust / 69

Under Jiu-yi Shan / 74

A Country without Names / 79

White Fire / 85

When the Quinces Begin to Ripen / 89

Flowering Midnight / 93

From Tide Washed Salterns / 100

The Carved Serpent / 102

Night / 104

Nostos / 108

Notes / 112

In Memory of Campbell Matthews

***

"In the 1920s British cellist Beatrice Harrison began practicing outdoors [and] nightingales ... began matching her arpeggios with carefully timed trills ... getting used to her they ... burst into song whenever she began to play. In 1924 ... the BBC [recorded her in her garden]. The duet was repeated live each year ... In 1942 ... the recording engineer hearing the droning sound of the beginnings of the Thousand Bomber raid on Mannheim shut off the sound ... A strange soundscape of menacing bombers and incessant nightingales singing ... in the midst of human destruction and violence."
—David Rothenberg, *Why Birds Sing*

***

Rock Star Celebrates Birthday at Exclusive Country House Retreat

Faint whiff of Grand Entrait, Clive Christian.
Beside the helipad, lake and gable-ivy ripple.
Subservient gravels crunch. The "proud, ambitious heap"
greets another well-heeled group. Round the inglenook
at dark babble of toasts under poster mock-up,
El Presidente, of birthday host. Looking down on
all the plunder, from Famagusta to Ferghana.
Finial, pediment, alabaster frieze: the frozen flight
from ennui. It's dead and scattered parts
cast in plaster, or bronze. A fixed expression
of a rapacious age. History narrating profit with loss.
Celebrity hedonists frolic amid its bric-a-brac.
Reluctant, atop their leafy sylvan slope, to engage
with what – head of walrus, polar bear, taxidermy
of arctic night – beyond all wealth, privilege
and power, might hold up before them
                                          a reproving gaze.

Road to the North

"Homeward you think we must be sailing
to our own land."
        Homer, *Odyssey* [X: 538-539]

I

Suddenly at the end of day, spectral tree blown
against the window, my father appears before me, marching
leading a shabby contingent of ghosts. They pause,
and then, the sound of half empty canteens
slopping at their waists, approach. I watch them, as if
through a stirred-up haze of dust, fragments
from a broken century, their laughter
and song drifting, as they march,
through time's porous and permeable borders
into our own, dissolving all horizons
and distances, shedding the dead weight
of months and years, to appear before
me, reinvigorated. Ghosts, feeding on my blood.

II

I ask him how they managed to arrive, unscathed
out of that gloom at the world's end. "Although
we summoned ourselves" he said "we were loath to
come back, knowing the way, that it would hold for us
only professed guilt. But for pity of you, and to see you
once again and warn you, before the clouds of darkness
block, finally, any hope of return ... On the way
by which we came, city after city, nothing but a heap
of smouldering stones, smoke, soot strewn mosques,
hospitals, bodies piled up on pavements, waiting.
As if entire countrysides and cities had been
offered up as burnt sacrifices to the god Mithra,
their odours pleasing to him. An ancient temple to him
preserved, parts of it, in the basement of the House
of Finance which, as we came closer to you,
we saw rising, all steel and glass, like a lance head
flashing under cloud, tilting at the very heavens
themselves. And all around us at night FIRE
the sleepers in untold doorways and hauling,
during day, bags stuffed with their possessions
from bench to low wall to under a bridge
out of the rain. Like those groups of vagabonds
listlessly adrift roaming the turnpikes after their land
was seized, their towns pulled down about their ears,
centuries ago. Home is always the testing ground for
cruelties we later export. In fading light we heard
the clank of uncoupled cars in the goods yards and,
from them, a low and muffled tune of despair. Its refrain
rang in our ears, hour after hour..."

III

He went on, measuring, carefully, his words: "Conscience, as we set out, compelled us to re-visit the very places where we had inflicted so much pain on others; not to relinquish to forgetfulness, by one ounce, the weight of our degeneracy. And to show you, in one broad sweep, both your inheritance and our burden. So we began where experience first indicted us ... Exhausted by heat, some apoplectic, we dropped like flies by the roadside, where they buried us. Our cemeteries marched with us, boon companions. Incised in stone, nameless –
most too low in rank to warrant more than 'private soldier' –
we were left behind; no loved ones who would come grieving for us later, on that road to the north, Uttarapath they call it, would be able to find where we lay. Wormsmeat. Slowly ingested and excreted; our boots laid with us in that night in case we might rise up and take again to walking…" And I thought I caught on the air, for one instant, the smell of stale sweat and moist leather, of scorching dust.

IV

Noticing the torn and scrofulous uppers
of their boots, I pitied them; that, stirring out of Erebus,
they'd had to traverse its smoke-filled chasms of
vaporous, blood-soaked roads to reach us. "My son" he said
"one need go no further than the nearest manhole and
pry off its lid, to let the fistula's dark stream that's
always under your feet, its rustling skin of vapours,
escape: here; where lies are roared out loud, where
the deepest vein of villainy is silence. The majority,
disdaining the stench, slam back the lid at once.
Few dare to linger over what so deeply offends
their sense of who they are: saviour or destroyer?
We are not, my son, what we so flatteringly imagine
ourselves to be. But comfort makes cowards of us all.
Let us continue, then, our blighted wanderings
so you may better grasp our burden, your inheritance…"

V

"At the edge of desert steppe were groves of date palms.
Dates and dung we called it: the camp. D and D. Knee deep
in dates. And camel dung: some rolled their cigarettes from it.
Little did we know what was to come. And in the evenings we fell
about to yarning about our days together on the Grand Trunk
Road. Said we remembered most the smells of spices and
incense intertwined with dust. Not that they weren't present
where we were. But less intense, varied. Remembered the
wayside shrines brightly bedecked, athrong with people. All that
colour, farrago of activity. And then the stillness, and the
silence after, in shadow under the banyan. A doze at midday,
when the sun was at its highest. Them – not us. Our boots
marching, always marching. And the dhaba, the road-side eateries.
Flatbreads crisping over coals. And onward it went, over fifteen
hundred miles, broad and smiling. Old hands from those parts,
with a smattering of Hindi, waxed lyrical (ah, nostalgia, it is a
dish one never tires of eating) about the coasts,
port-cities where their fathers settled and traded. Where,
bunnias told them, even the parrots once spoke in five languages
when the trade routes were open and flourished. But
where, last century, when our presence became too much
of a burden to them, all that remained were soot blackened
burnt out bungalows and stations. And then gallows.
Lynchings that went on for years. Every 'nigger' (one old hand
mimicked the distress on the bunnia's face) they came
across strung up. Shot. Or bayoneted. Man. Woman. Child…"

VI

"Years later, chest deep in water, waiting
for the small boats to ferry us, ranged out
along the shore, all I could think of was sand
and the abandoned roads which, after we'd
disembarked at Haifa, ran off into it,
the settlements and villages which we pulled
down without compunction. And those we left
standing, bereft, without a home or food
or means of subsistence, in their own country."
His eyes lowered upon his hands, as if suddenly
they had become the seat of all impurity,
transgression, and stayed there a long time, even
after he resumed talking. "And even later still,
many years on, after we had left that cold, grey
northern coast, re-posted to another, warmer
country, in their eyes whenever they met ours,
in their pained look of scrutiny, I was reminded." Again
he stopped, again looked at his hands. "Of what?"
I asked. "Of fear. In our own. That went
unacknowledged. Of the order, months later,
to burn. Burn all the crates. So many of them.
Crammed with files. And to rake, and re-rake, all
the waste, reduced, already, to ash. And to make
sure nothing of it survived that was not
"broken up". Fear. Theirs, that gave the order.
And ours. In a crateful of ash. So desperate
to extinguish what, in all those records of
organised violence and inhumanity, proved us inferior
to those we slanderously depicted as inferior
to ourselves. Fear. Of exposure, and of obloquy…"

VII

Another of the regiment, flaxen haired, still with the
cloud of an untimely death about him, who,
with my father, had survived to reach the beaches
where they stood waiting to be taken off, but who,
weakened by fatigue and cold, had drowned before
they could haul him aboard, spoke, in a lifting Antrim
accent: "We were, like someone wrote, no more
than uniformed assassins. Nothing we, or our leaders,
did could atone for the misery we'd inflicted
on so many innocent of any crime but trying to live
in their own country ruled by their own kind.
Fleeing, later, through the city where most of us
would eventually embark, I stumbled onto the black
cobblestones, tripped by a fallen wire. All the
telegraph lines were down. Your father helped
me up and I limped off, half walking/trotting
and looking frequently back for any sign of the
pursuer who, at that very moment, was doing no more,
or less, than we had for untold years been doing –
crossing the borders of a sovereign country in force
to take and claim it as our own. And in some cases,
where they wouldn't put up with it, exterminating
them." He shivered. Then shuffled. Tugged his collar
up... "In truth", my father concurred "it could be said
that before we were the victims of those who
pursued us, we were their accomplices, preparing
the ground for the horrors that were to come..."

VIII

At first light I saw my father's figure at the window
against the stirring undulations of lace, wavering,
bending with them from a breeze out of darkest
Erebus, and shedding that semblance of solidity
it had retained for the journey to us. As I moved
towards him his form stabilised. I drew back.
"We'll soon be gone" he said. "Here, fear bred out of greed,
bred out of loss of trust, urged us, dead spirits, back. 'Thieves
and liars' we were called, when living. Justly. For that
our souls daily scald, simmer on burning sand, on live
coals." The window rattled to a violent gust, pushing
the pane in then drawing it back. "Put no faith in good
works. They only paper over cracks. It's here", pointing to
his chest, "work's done. Here alone. Trust no one's word.
But when they act, weigh stated intent with consequence
– to see if they are one. That way you'll drive out the rat
beneath the pile. A lifetime's work. You'll get
little help. Good luck … Here, from what we've seen,
perjury, in all spheres of public life, is not a crime.
So with the law at large, home and abroad. Ignored.
Bent. Or remade. To fit the purposes of the rich, the
powerful … The day after they wrenched that flagstaff from
the lawn in front of Government House, sweating and silently
cursing, they merely thrust and planted it in another
land. Later, in another form. Right through the heart.
Masters of deception. Their trade. From 'Empire' to
'Commonwealth'. Mere name-change: "To smell
much sweeter in the public nose." But, at the end of day,
the only ones such trade truly benefits are their own…"

IX

"Here all the oracles have fallen silent.
All the shrines, and their *genius loci*, have
been abandoned. All the observances,
the oblations. All ancient ritual,
supervising terror. The desert's getting
nearer and nearer." I watched my father as he
pondered us. Alienated sojourners. Worshippers
of false idols. He saw us, clandestinely
nurtured by a state intent on preventing us
identifying common purpose, straying out of
our dried-up paths into ruinous ideological
postures. Narrow doctrinal, sentimental
utopias of political propriety. Thirsters
whom the thirst disfigures, distorts.
On our city walls and our street corners
he saw only the graffiti of a corrupted
faith. After he left I dreamed I saw him, and
his shabby contingent, again, walking
through the twilight dust of Uttarapath,
as if they were walking through a sacred
grove, far from what they'd experienced
here: rubble and spolia. Our chthonic
shrines long since dismantled and buried
beneath a network of motorways and malls.

X

In the dead of winter, now, I return, to the
pitted granite of his headstone, tilting
on the small bluff above the river, as if
blown crooked by the wind which always blows
here. Beneath me, through thin aspen and alder,
the dust of a suburban Sahara moves on the air
above shallow marsh embankments, darkening
against the edge of a sky grey as that half-
light moving up out of the river, and I know
there will not be another nekuia, that
"[we] will never find that life for which
[we] are looking." A drowsy congregation,
laity of restless consumers, easily distracted
by each latest invention; deferential, mindlessly
concordant with our "sowre complexion[ed]" clergy
in its towers of steel and glass, rising
above us. Victims of a corrosive insecurity,
we sail off into the future never looking
back; unable to ascertain, alienated
from repetition, a rhythm, a pattern, a music
woven into the air and the earth and
heart which beats in accordance with it.

Alder

"'Everything is eternal, yet nothing is constant.' The entire landscape …
is a nexus of Power moving beneath the outward appearance of things
… of Persons shifting in and out of form, of patterns recombining."
        Ruth Holmes Whitehead, *Mi'kmaw Legends*

I

That look in each other's eye. Brief
moment of terror. Foreboding.
On the road we did not follow.
In the field we did not plough.
At the quay from which we never departed.

Instead of assarts, palisadings:
the dust-filled spoor, the chewed stem.
Interpreting the sign. In the night
the sound of our fire in the wind.
An ember, a bone. Cracking.

Pale blossoms trickling our faces.
Feathering air. Listening to names.
Of those who wandered off into towns
and cities. Those who did not return.

II

Branch against branch.
Squeaking. In wind round
the fire at night. Rubbing.
Or is it the longspur, again,
in the deep wood, calling?

A cold wind screams
through the emptiness
of asylums. From far off.
We hear it. In the snow
that is falling. We cannot
make out our breath.
Or the tracks of
the animals that
                are leaving.

What if we should arrive in a place
we have not been in before.
A place whose guardians we
might have offended. Bearing,
in our arms, no gifts
of conciliation. Searching,
under drifts, for last year's shoots.
Listening. For a pattern, a rhythm?

At night, in the deep wood.
At year end. In the dark. Chanting.
Alder. Bear's blood. Sap
of the ministrating moon.
A circuit. In the roots
the figure of a man. Breathing.

III

That song. Heard once deep
in the wood. Not forgotten.
Celebrating. *Something must
leave for something to return.*
To hold the breath, as security,
for a perpetual bequest. For
the re-turns flesh rejoices in.

Where nothing, beyond the
staked out boundary, seems
to be what it appears to be.
Like smoke, in and out
of branches. Vestment,
of many unfoldings. Pausing.
Coming and going. A trail,
with signs on it. Fragrant
with possibility.
                We walk on it.

Scent of dry grass, scorched dust.
Silence sifted. Tenuous note.
Weaving through branches. Heard,
and not followed. Followed
and lost. To where night leads.
In shadow. Eater and eaten.
Surmounting terror. In solvents
of the long dawn that follows.
                              Touch.

IV

Tracks of Ursus, in the cold
night sky above us. Crunch
of snow in the deep wood.
Crack of frozen branches.
Prey and pursuer, in an
imperishable pattern, wheeling
on their axis. Above the ebb
and flow and tumult endless
ly spread out beneath them.

One night, after many nights, in a wild place
amid sunken roots and sounds, of scattered shapes
and shadows, alone, and wrestling with phantoms
the marching minute hand of time, a fool's errand
and burden, cutting out shapes from nothing
to do its bidding, fell away and I could hear,
through rustling foliage, smell and see at last,
beneath that fluid vestment of its being
in which it had been cast, one part bear and

one part person, the vision move toward me.
That other shape and dwelling in which my own
shape could not last, overwhelmed and then,
as earth inhales and exhales our shadow,
released me. Seven nights it came, with a gentle
rustling of foliage, to where I lay or sat.
And stopped and looked for a long time at me.
Its gaze inquisitive, penetrating. And then I knew,
at almost its last visit, what it was thinking:
'So you too would wear the clothes of a bear. And I,
too, in them, could come and sit beside your fire.
And neither you, nor I, would let the other go hungry'.

Through cold taut air we look up
under a canopy of startled stars.
The Great Bear above us, at
the still centre of the revolving
world. Moves, pivots through
the night sky and, again, we follow.

In the deep shadow under the tree.
In the rubble of scattered stones,
bits of bark and earth, within it.
Known, but not heard. Heard, but not
seen. In fragments of birdsong.
All day. All night. Arising. Because
each thing is, in some way, united.
Within the shadow of the tree. Moving.
Amongst the living and the dead.

Envoys and emissaries. Of
an indestructible energy. Gained
and spent, transferred and
assimilated, dissipated. Only,
again, to be renewed. Elusive
divinities, circling us round the fire
at night. Circling, in a never
ending inhalation, exhalation.
Keeping it going. A rhythm,
                        a pattern.

And those who breathe, in
the shadow. Wait. Hold back.
In the flickering half-light.
Understand. Terror in their eyes.
The Forms. The passing procession.
Then raise their voices. Chanting.
At year end. Under the alders.
                Keeping it going.

V

In the deep wood, all day long,
the call of the longspur. But
fewer and fewer of us each
year, many wandering off into
towns and cities, to hear it.

Only a cold wind through
the trees. Only the wind
shaking boughs, weaving
through far off asylums,
through empty lots and
run down malls. And the rain.

Driven Dust

[*Some surviving fragments from an unofficial account recorded by a temple scribe at Uruk during the reign of Rim-Anum. It consists of observations by a man captured in a military campaign to procure corvée labour from amongst 'unadministered' gathering hunting and fishing communities south of Uruk.*]

"O the folly of you who follow each day the furrow, knee deep in milk, semen and dung, sweating in the dark byre. Hacking the rock face. In the deep tunnel. Or tethered for months upon plains, bitten by black fly, counting (#3)

Constructors of storage pits, grain houses you dream under a starless roof. Proclaimers of omens and auguries, always genuflecting, praying, organising offerings. Anxiously measuring hours, days. Your calendars do not console you. (#5)

By eating your fear you do not rid yourselves of it. At your shrines where sacrifices are performed, in your lavishly wrought Hall of Administrators, you confirm and endorse it. Then manipulate and, for your own profit, exploit it. (#11)

You look down on us. 'You're driven dust: over the hills and through the trees, creeks and marshes' you say. 'Children. Never settling in one place long enough. Drinkers of unclean water.'" (#8)

Where No Snow Falls

"Rosy-fingered Dawn has broken her coloured pencils. Now they lie scattered about like nestlings with empty, gaping beaks."
        Osip Mandelstam, *The Egyptian Stamp*

It was clear to their companions
before they left, from ominous mutterings
about 'this bordello of a world',
that their journey was not to
extend love, or understanding.
But to gratify avarice. A boy's dream.
To arrogate dominion, practice cruelty.

Headstrong, they were unable
to restrain them from leaving.
For coasts where scent of cedar
carried many miles out to sea
to them. For shores where charcoal
burners waited, their fires raising
dark clouds turning noon into night:
where apparitions appeared before
them, phalloi round their necks,
striding with outstretched arms.

Under a brine damp bluff.
Embers of logs. Charred bones
of offerings. Spilled lustral water.
Wine. On the beach, beside the quay,
dark stain of caulking. As they departed
they called out to those on the shore:
"We are the voice of Man apart.
We speak the language,
the triumphant tongue, of History."

*Those who stand, the dispossessed,
by the roadside. Abayas fraying beneath
loads. In driving sand. Sun glare.
Clutching pots and pans. Listening
to far off explosions. Neither forgotten.
Nor acknowledged. Live on, in the black
wind at the horizon. In a broken-
floored orphanage. Beside a rusting
swing. Gate with hinges twisted.*

Above salt-caked tholepins
dead bird pinned in a forestay
its cries unheard. In thresh of wind's fury.
In wave surge, counter-surge.
"The land where no snow falls,
nor long frost of winter." On slithery
benches. Recited, over and over.
Amidst loosening breakers.
Embroidered on each foaming ridge.

Endless, sea-choked divagations.
Skins salt, wind scoured.
Days and nights outlasting
tempests. Hauled, to the
precipice's edge. Dropped. Years.
Thinking. Back to an old quay
by a fleece-scrub headland
and a glorious welcome. Cool
shade of laurel at the well. Sweet
smell of broom. Sound of
woodpecker in copse of hazel.

Others in leaking boats,
wash up on perilous reefs.
Or in the deep sea, wallowing.
Overcrowded. Young and old.
Fleeing each decimated village.
With little water. Less food.
Requesting sanctuary. Their cities
in flames. Some drowning
in sight of those same lands
from which the despoilers
                        had set out.

Mid-day heat: desiccated air.
Dust. Chirr of cicada. On the
deeply wooded ascent slow sound
like water. Breeze rippling
leaves. On the bleached track
no footprint. Beside a grey clump
of olive trees, high on a scarp
of crumbled rock, they located
the shrine, and the oracle...
'To have climbed this far
is to have mistaken the sound
of longing for the sound of water.
For what you would quench
you need not have travelled so far'

Reliquary

(For James Hamilton-Paterson)

"He who has gone beyond … who
has crossed to the other shore."
Dhammapada [26: 414]

Nameless land. Haunting the salt marsh
and the ridges above it. Where
my childhood is a shimmering chip
washed from the stream's bed.
A latent pattern, a tendency. But
no point of rest. No permanent object.

To carry sorrow with one. From the very
beginning. On the worn trackway. From
the moss boughed orchard's proffered vowels.
Through cuttings of wounded field maple.
To
    the sound of fracture.
    Of necessary distance.

And the light said: "There is no necessary distance. To follow the teloi in the stream's bed, anticipate nothing. Listen to birds call above the silted wharf, its timbers cracked and rotting. Can you discern from their flight where desire and goal co-incide?"

To negotiate, always, a modified terrain.
To refuse the words. To break the circuit
of appropriation. So the pattern falters.
                    Only to be re-traced.
In the ordinary conversation. Indicating
a point of reference. Concealing
                    a necessary silence.

Mossed boughs move in wind
through a sediment of syllables.
Of projected attributes, fears, needs.
Our universal categories. Perfecting
a man, woman. And the stream seeps
into the parched ground at their feet
like a stain. Carrying them forward.

But the sorrow remained:
on the faded trackway,
strewn with blossom, a way of ancient
conciliatory voices. Unobscured under
the weight of their intoning.

At the edge of water.
When leaves were falling.
After the first insults,
    woundings.
Air hardened.
    Light faltered.
In the unbroken circuit.
The world doubled.

And the pattern persisted. Daily.
In thousands of 'disownings', appropriations.
Until the necessary feint was infolded,
included in the act. And the distance
became a mandatory deception.

*
* *
*

Washed from the stream's bed.
Shining white chip. My shadow
beside me. Into the broken world
of sound and sense. Into the tangled
maze nestled at the salt marsh's
edge. Inaudible. Invisible. Until in it.

Sound coveted. Sense commanding.
A systematic link. A pattern
between sound and meaning. Across
an infinite variety of sounds and meanings.
Supplanter, discreditor of silence.
Of that syntax of what can't be said.

In the orchard
    sound of a swing
moving in wind.
    Empty.
        Voices.
Moving among trees.
            "There
    is nothing,
apart from the expression,
    to be expressed."

    A swing.
    Moving. Moved.
        In wind.
Beyond you. Beyond
    all sound
            words.

   After the alteration
of air to accept what the ear,
assimilated in the pattern,
commended to your attention.
                             After
  the end of birdsong.
On the faded trackway by
the ashwood you heard,
       dance
  of leaf / dust,
in the shadows' dry
             asseveration,
    nothing.

*
* *
 *

Under flowering dogwood. New-laid topsoils
held sediment of brick, beam. Reliquary
of plaster, wallpaper, bone. Debris of Doodlebug,
incendiary. Barges, heavy with it.
Past Shoreditch, Gravesend. Entering
the Lower Hope. Dim, charnel water
that the stream, from its sand-capped
scarp where you dangled feet, daily fed.

Into your cuff-frayed hand, snow wrapped,
a letter, indissoluble judgement handed down:
to an Inferior Person.
    Years later, recalling
job interviews, its repeated indictment.
In their ears a coarse-grained accent.
Assembly line future. Honorarium of ditches,
doffing. Plate full of
                cold potatoes.

Fracas outside the gates. Bludgeon
of wood to right femur. Blood
stained kerbstone, resistant
to erasure. Inside, after the bell had gone,
simmering quiescence. Touching of breast.
Trouser pocket of hardness. Subject
transformed,
          into hapless object.

Slowly, noiselessly over the years,
under the dogwood,
the drip and seep, through untold
strata. Drip and seep. Noiseless
   accruing.

    Marsh marigold
        flowering rush,
  infiltrate
substitute themselves for
each object. By the ashwood,
on the trackway murmurous
with voices. The pattern
prevails, the circuit is
    unbroken.
               Always,
    a little further
a little more estranged
from where you are
from where the moment
    occurs, undiverted.

    Beneath the parched
    sand-scarp, by dried out
banks of silt, the wharf
timbers, quietly, are
    warping
            cracking.

But beneath the ridge, on that faded
trackway when the sound of the voices was
almost unheard above the shift of wind
through thin salt mists drifting northward
your shadow returned, beside the ashwood,
                             to remind you.

And the light said: "Anticipate nothing."
On a gatepost a bird sang.
And, for a moment, the pattern was
interrupted. In the silence that ensued
there was another, deeper, silence
                        haunting the ridges.
Without which you could not proceed.

   At the heart
of the dis-continuous present
the sensation (verbally silent)
  of birdsong
   not birdsong itself

that which could not
  be heard:
     name   letter
       mouth
  ful only   of a
                    ir

※
※ ※
※

In the orchard, where you left
your name incised in bark. In
each honeyed vowel. In the mossed
sediment of syllables upon
each branch, their accrued
appetencies, the weight of darkness
and sweetness. There the swing moves,
still, of its own accord. Empty.
In a wind emptied. Full
                        of silence.

Midsummer fires along the ridge
where you wandered, a pebble
from the stream's bed in your palm,
warming what once was molten
turning it over and over.
Memory of fire. Bright flicker
of water, flame. Fused
                        brick
    and bone.

Apple blossom, leaf
   air fragrant
with them,
     the sound of sense
          ripening
  on the tongue,
    consume
and console what,
    ultimately, cannot
  ever return
            to what was
apple blossom

     l
       e
    a
       f

Drip
       of dew
   from the tall blades
       of grasses
   at the salt marsh's edge.
       In the stillness
           which moves
   out across sea embankments.
       In the unexpiated light
           which drains
   from the estuary's mouth.
               Drip.

       Drip.

*
* *
*

At sand-capped scarp
stream hard as glass
                        snow
piled high on trackway
bereft of voices, on
the quiet inlet below.

                 A lone figure
  on the shore:
motionless, in a place erased
of mark or sign, white
as snow continually falling
straining to look
            to the further shore.

Uncomfortably at Home

(*i.m.* Randal Bingley)

Out of their broken shadows they emerge
trees, much as they were, fixed years ago
in a sepia image of this Thameside village.
I stand on its descending road, where
in 1381 Tomas Baker ignited a countrywide
rebellion attacking poll-tax commissioners
collecting revenue for more foreign wars.
Liberally, richly festooned now with litter
of a nation hopelessly addicted to endless
consumption. Swept clean each day by
an array of cleaners, remunerated by
a state grown wealthy from centuries
looting overseas possessions. Where
the road ends at an earthen sea-wall
a sailing-barge sits, still, on a sepia evening
in 1909, on or off-loading at high water
in the lay-by of a wharf now vanished.

The trees shake down on me a dusty
pallor: consequence of that moment
standing when young before for the
first time the strange swaying motion of
their beauty. Wanting, but being unable,
to surrender to it. To trees, tideway and
village: habitat of one who, bereft
of qualifications, felt trapped beside a tidal
waste, targeted as raw material, provider of
surplus. A feeling that festered. Leading me
to put thousands of miles between it and

myself. Metic, for decades, under tropical sun.
No longer sucked down among a class content
to sink not swim, kept docile with a few stale
tidbits, a day off each week, an employer's
annual seaside outing, while in Westminster
they gulped subsidised wine and meat.
And what if I'd remained, instead, at home
looking out over the dammed-off navigable
tideway that had effected an entrance to the
village once, amid those trees, and people
many whose names, not faces, I have forgotten,
and so much else, in this country whose
history, so much of it, happened overseas?
But to have returned, to have become
domesticated once more to the violence
of that history, of its ruinous expropriations
overthrowing of governments, torture
pauperisation and death, would have been
       not to have left at all.

On a raw December evening shadows
sweep into a dusty stand of trees
topping the bluff, rattling churchyard gate
dimming headstone inscriptions of family,
pilots who traversed these treacherous tidal
flats, and I hear, immobilised within a maze
of mud and water, their sighs. They echo
along channels. Over embankments guiding
the inlet's flow where I've wandered mind
navigating an endless historical discourse
of incorporation and exclusion, corroborating
neither. Under trees, now, I stand beside a leafless
road and pick a stray white hair from my collar.

Then turn my head out of the wind that blows
across the long grey waste of channels.
In the autumn air a presentiment of snow.

Road of Dust

"The north wind rolls the white grasses and breaks them."
                                              Ts'en Ts'an

I

Deep red, still, leaves in winter. Edged
white with frost. By the stone pond in the east
courtyard. They chitter, stiff as husks, in
the wind. Within it the stink of blood.
By the south wall the willows are grieving.
Corpses pile up in alleys and on streets.
No one has the strength to bury them.
A bushel of rice now fetches ten thousand
copper coins. In the dead of night the sound
of rats rummaging. Of owls, hunting.

II

Beside Clear Mind Pavilion wind
blows cold. Over terraces of jasper
balustrades of marble, in the east
courtyard. Over all accumulations of
dissimilar, successively disappearing
moments onto which we hold. Extinguishing
fires of inured appetency. I listen.
To silence. To the chanting of
sutras over the lichened steps
under the eaves as we depart, at day-
break. Pale smoke of wild cherry blossom
hovers on trees in the courtyard.

III

The journey north. Digesting hard roads.
Admonished, stoking factional
deliberations, by our griefs. Surprised.
In the wheel's smouldering nave, on
the dust-thronged axletree, we hear
the smoking world revolve. The crack
of it, day after day, in each ice-dark rut.
Its iron rim sinking. Then rising. And
the flutter and quivering rasp, in the cob's
nose and mouth, of air. Caught in its mane
a cloud of spangled sweat is freezing.

IV

At the Mingde Gate wind blows
cold. And colder. We wait. The folds
of our garments stiffen. Words
in our mouths grow heavy with the weight
of surrender. In a white line beneath
the persimmon trees – attired as if for a
funeral. We shiver. Biding his time,
with a long retinue of retainers,
languidly, Taizu drifts toward us. Uncouth,
with an imperious gaze, and no ear
for music. Except the disorganized sound
of battle. Behind him, in weak winter light,
gleam of deep azure finials. I run
my tongue around my mouth, trying to dispel
sourness of weeks of incarceration.

V

Voices of bargemen from the canal:
poling and exhorting as, slowly, with a
cargo of salt from the coast, they pass.
Sounds from teahouses and carriages
thread streets of the south quarter. Peddlers
hawk quinces beside the outer courtyard.
I shut my eyes in early morning glare.
Mind drifts. Shadows of marble and jasper
float. Broken. Sifted. A stream: of
accumulations. Of name and form. "The world
is only names". A corvée trudges to the canal
to dredge and haul till dusk all its dark filth.
The smell of it will hang for days on the air
filling the inner courtyard and rooms.

VI

Alone at the end of day. I lean on
the balcony gazing south, in dust that's
whirled from the dried out floodplain.
It stings my eyes. To my many titles now
Taizu has added another. Marquis of Wei
Ming: of Disobeyed Edicts. To tighten
the knot of my humiliation. In twelve
months: mother: milk-son: wife. Gone.
New, young wife, forced to his pleasure.
All night unable to sleep: across the
courtyard incense silently drifts
coiling, rippling blue scarves.
And a bulbul, hearing the smoking
world revolve, sings in the abandoned temple
overhung with willows beside the canal.

VII

From an imbroglio of dust and wind
in the inner courtyard, suddenly,
there came a faint and acrid smell,
like that of fish staled in warp
and weft of clothing. A man. Walking
out of the shadows. With a dirt stained
face, shouldering a basket. Zheng Wenbao.
Disguised. Last seen months before
by the stone pond in the east courtyard
where we had gathered. And then, in the
time it seems to take a gust of
wind to rise and pass, he was
gone. But from the long interlude
of our conversation, his astute eye
and speech penetrating the depths
of my condition, lodged in my mind, stayed,
his words: "Forget Jinling".

VIII

Amid unfamiliar smells, shapes, this
far north: shadows lengthen, deepen.
On the wind, for a moment, sounds
like chanted sutras. The bulbul
sings again from the ruined temple.
At all the river crossings, in my sleep,
the dead raise their heads. More
than a hundred thousand. In mud
their banners rot. Shrouds for hungry
orphans, widows. By the east courtyard
they lingered. Or flocking like phantoms

to the road, collapsed: too weak to
continue. Listening, there, to the
smoking world revolve. Deep in its iron
groove. And the scent of wild cherry
blossom overflowed the east courtyard.

Under Jiu-yi Shan

"I now state my terms to the crocodiles. I set them a limit of three days to take their ugly selves south to the sea … Do not repent when it is too late!"
                Han Yu, *Address to the Crocodiles of Chaozhou*

I

By the east lake the wind blows hard.
Over reed marsh, mud flat and shallow.
Tundra swan, stork and crane already
have landed. Out of that far barbarian
heaven where snow falls and falls without
stopping. Where, leaving, day after day they heard
nothing but the sound of wind through passes,
across ice-locked rivers, sweeping
the slightest hint of warmth before it.
At the lake edge I stand. Listening. Sedge, crisp
with frost, under my feet crunches. Wondering
at how winter has arrived so early.

II

On Great Marsh of Cloud Dream, alone,
I compose verses, to which no one will listen.
The court of Chu puff themselves up,
parade around, bristle. Idle and poisonous
chatter is all they engage in: a quagmire
of lies, vilifications and distortions
discrediting those who seek to curtail
their orgies of nepotism and licence.
They would, if they had to,
fill a bag of flowers with excrement
and proclaim that it smells fragrant.

They'd rather, I am sure, that I obliged
by falling into a river full of crocodiles
than ever reappearing amongst them. On
Great Marsh of Cloud Dream I chant
and the birds accompany me, migrants
from far lands, in a music of impending chaos.

III

Mist rolls in over muddy flag filled bottoms.
A rufous sandstone cloud erupts
from the lake's bed, when the foot's
thrust in it. A darkening pandemonium.
Beside me sweet caneflower-
silvergrass leans and shivers. Cold
October air. Wisps linger and curl
over long silt-spits that glisten half submerged.
From creek-head to creek-head the sound
of rites. Drumming. Drumming.
Unabated. Each nubile waist
encircled by an arm. Dancing and
pursuing in flux and twist of air and
water the whirlwind and the storm. To ease
the dried out heart. To atone. Old
crocodile skin, stretched under the
hand, whose broken lachrymose fate
is conjured and elucidated in your note?

IV

Eaten under the shade of
Jiu-yi Shan, in dark water
close to Burned Field Village.
At the placid, lapping margin.
So completely devoured, no sign

of them remaining. In each loose-reign
prefecture I ride through, carts loaded.
Families adrift on the roads. Sour
smelling, brackish the taste of a life
lived under Jiu-yi Shan. Far out
the sound of a storm brews over the water.
Muffled, intermittent rumbling.
I listen. Leaves of the orchid
tremble. Fleabane glimmers at the water's
edge, damp from a low cloud that hangs
heavily above it. In the air, scent
of cassia. Over the south running channels.
I point my horse's head toward them.
With a stumble, and a sigh, we follow.

V

Within a charred circle of thoroughwort
ash of incense and powdered bone.
Impress of makeshift shrine, dismantled.
Cloud black over vastness of water sky all
the way back to Ying. The damp wind spawns
sinister phantoms that writhe and twist
their way into the heart, when one is
not looking. Sinuous as guts of sacrifice
spread out and interpreted. But who
is the one who yields the life, and the
one who takes it? The sanctimonious cant
of those who thrive, courtiers covetous
of their own comfort and security, only drives the
knife deeper. I came upon this bloodstained
spot at evening, my horse exhausted
my stomach cramped with hunger, long after
the rites had ended. Behind me
from scattered bivouacs of those from

Chu who'd fled, rather than remain to see
the coming disaster, smoke was rising.

VI

The Imperial Inquisitors of Chin, a country
of wolves and tigers, sit in their gold
plated palanquins and dispense
injustice. Connoisseurs of terror their fingers whiten
often. No room for treatises on music,
philosophy or history in the Imperial
Archive. They burn them. And no need
to bury your head in the sand – they
will, if you write or read such nonsense,
do it for you. Or get someone else to:
there's never any shortage of hoodlums
among us. Each night paranoia stalks their bed-
chambers. Informers in every household. Too
many to unmask: who would unmask them?
When the wind blows south, over the
Han River, it is full of black dust.
Cities, townships and villages. Burning.
Slowly, it filters down upon us.

VII

Waste of protectorates, of vassals.
North of the Han River. A cold wind
cracks the faces, tears the banners of
Chin armies. But still they move south
ward devouring, like a silk worm, leaf
upon leaf. Massing on our borders.
Pretending it is we who are threatening
theirs. What can't be expropriated
by force they expropriate by trickery and

deception. Chin Shih Huang-ti, face of
jackal breast of bird of prey, has torn off
the cankered flesh of our court, bit by bit.
Gnawed through its heart. So easy to destroy
such credulous self-flattering fops
trading gold and precious stones for enslavement
to a corrupt bureaucracy of sycophants
willing to do anything for advancement.
So it has been since ancient times. Why
do I complain that men are blind today?
Jin Shang, Cheng Hsiu, Tzu Lan. May
you consume what you have harvested.

VIII

All the fragrant leaves have withered.
Orchid, sun-apple, white rumex, cart-halting
flower, sweet spirit grass. Fleabane bends
back in the wind. Over the muddy bottom
under Jiu-yi Shan my reflection wavers.
Words, like stones, sink. On the air strange accents.
From far prefectures northward. From a
government geared for war, not peace: women tilling
fields, men away expanding borders. Outlaws
in the forests and marshes. I raise my head.
A faint drumming over dark waves. The wind
blows hard. Cold hands lift cold water to
parched lips. White as thistledown my breath.
Suddenly all the birds are leaving.

A Country without Names

"To whom there are no accumulations, who have comprehended the nutriments, and whose range is the deliverance of the 'void' and 'signless' – their track is as hard to trace as that of birds in the sky" —*Dhamapada* [7: 92]

"And yesterday we will arrive"
he had said "in a country without names.
Where the past, decorated and mutilated,
will confront us on every street corner,
begging for alms and bread, veteran
of many wars and atrocities, coughing
in shop doorways at night, cold
with the stale sweat and weight of
a soiled historiography, cult of idols,
under its head. And nothing but a baleful
choir of cats and ghosts to sing it to sleep."

~ ~

Wisp of fragrance
on the air. Jasmine
or orange. As from
an unseen garden. Here
where they advanced,
crossing the narrow strait
wreathed in sea fog,
at the Western edge
of the world. Days,
long stretched out
to year end,
of carrion and blood.
Of dead gods. Their
names unrecited.

～～
        Broken,
    haunted ground.   All
  previous moments   endure:
    afternoons devoured
by almanacs   uprooted gardens
    of shadows smoke
        and blood
      flower again.
  A bird sings :   the reality
of a single, unifying moment
                      before words.
    Amid querulous
    apparitions
                  days
    move.

～～

On the river, vapours tangle
ghostly rigging: bullion, gold plate,
coin. Undisturbed,
along with ensign and
corpse, buried. As we walk past
we hear, from houses
on the embankment
packed with benches, the rancid patter
of deodorized words. Abuzz
above a technology of extirpation.

～～

               Tumescence
of word on morning steps.
                              Rustle
of newsprint as we breathe
      in the air
                 events
taking place around us. Near
    and far. It is only
background music. The sound
    of the times:
         a "polluted vehicle".
Day and night, it rolls over us.
   The voice, always,
of the revisable moment
     lost too soon,
                never
   recovered.
                 Frozen
footprints on a lawn.
                   A bird calling.

             ~ ~

Wisp of fragrance
on the air,
in the moonlit street,
as from
an unseen garden. There
memory moves,
                   across
a waste expanse
of collapsed columns
statues, where
under motionless palms

*leaning
against fragments,
"actuated only by the
love of order and
justice" they "advance[ ]
towards perfection."*

~ ~

What did we see,
walking with our heads down,
beyond that gallery of "broken
statues and [...] tragic columns"
assembled line of legends
and heroes?
In a state,
from the very beginning,
of denial, the dead word,
proposing everything
& affirming nothing,
pressed upon our tongue
in a shadowy
consecration:
a counterfeit obolus
to ferry us across
the creaking river-ice
to an embankment of buried
skulls and voices.

~ ~

Who "can change the attitude of
those with power [...] make himself heard?"
Through ruined orchards, in desolate
provinces, amid charred palms
fragments of staircases, scorched walls,
the chimera beckons: 'This way. This way.
Here there is gold, there is oil, there
is sugar, all manner of things we don't have,
or in insufficient quantity.' The moon

shines on sleeping forms in doorways.
As it always will. Those gods, their shrines
a fine dust on the antennae of cities, on
whom we might have called in a moment
of doubt, anticipating terror, have departed.
Leaving only, at blossoming sepulchres, dignitaries
bending the knee, adopting obligatory poses.

~ ~

    What are they for
                words
gods of an omnipotent country
on a station platform in winter
  reading the signs
             at a bank counter
calculating advantage and loss
or in the great clearing house
of the supramundane
              drawn
upon all of us
        sooner or later
    taken into account.

~ ~

       Birds cross the sky.
       Silent above
us as we lift our heads to watch
      them. They depart
for a place unspecified
       undetermined.   A country
without names.
              Fleetingly
    their shadows write
on kerbstones at the corner of the street
where we stand. Our heads turn
      to follow a track
           we can only dimly
make out. Returning again
    to where we stand.
                 Foot
on kerb. Hand on familiar shoulder.
      Listening.
To someone trying again to write
    our history.
  Trying to call the birds back.

White Fire

"Vain to listen to the love song which a ghost sadly sings"
—Li Shang-Yin

I

In a seaside resort,
bereft of family
friends, a migrant
from war-torn lands
dreams of bunch grass
in fierce light
blowing before a door.
A white fire.

*

Warm wind full of ghosts.
Scent of lemon blossom.
But no lemon blossom.
Shadow land
through which he walks
meeting his shadow
coming back.

*

At a cross roads
amid spent bullet
casings, discarded fan-
belts and tyres
someone is reciting
a prayer
and someone is crying

the name
of a town or village
to which they do not
know how to return.

*

Crepuscular forms
asleep in shop doorways
bus shelters.
Moved on.
Tumbleweed lives.
Trudging at dawn
past newsagent billboards
announcing more foreign wars.

*

A shadow moves
from ridge to ridge.
A dark fluttering
of birds. History
is what happens far
off. Across a lawn

onto patio steps
lilac scent drifts
on summer nights.

*

Warm wind full of ghosts.
One returns, always,
to a memory. A steppe
of ruined horizons.

Smoke. Dense,
drifting. At dusk, saltwort:
little pink flowers.
Rut and hummock.
And only bitter water to drink.

II

No shrapnel-severed dream
here. Just broken limbs
of trees after the storm, debris from
overturned bins of garbage, oily fume
of skunk from two rough sleepers, wind-
blown wraiths, shadows, in
a shelter on the front. Fresh print
of gull on sand. He bends above it
and sees, looking around, his own
print where he approached. Its ragged,
fluctuant track. And tries, softly
intoning, to call back a ghost.

*

Above the sound of waves, distant
rustle of scrub, faint first breeze rippling
desert steppe. Working the mind
again. Its broken door. Well-head full
of sand. Its threadbare rope that goes
clack, clack, clack. With nothing at the end
of it. Except a dusty road, white as worm-
wood under midday sun. Black shadows
on it. Chafed feet. Burnt and torn.

*

Friday night. Eviscerated black
plastic bags. Gulls scavenge
gutter and road. Pier lights
orderly, in regular sequence, wink
on a sea always changing,
always dark. Outside a corner pub
men drink and talk. Stumbling,
later, to pee in the alley behind.
They return to smoke. He glances
at them as he wanders
back to his room. Sea spray
blows into his face. Small puddles
form as he walks. Pausing only to
lift off the counter's formica top,
a cuisine not tried before,
dinner in a styrofoam box
and then to consume, its words
a pulp he spits out,
fortune's complimentary cookie.

*

Warm wind full of ghosts.
Bunch grass blowing before
a door. As white as fire
or phosphorous combustible like
the morning star. As nights draw
in travel agent windows scream:
'Depart'! Everyone packs for the sun.
And, stepping over a puddle, he can
almost smell the scent of lilac that's
to come, that will call them back
again to grill, patio, lawn. There,
punctuated by the popping of corks,
the smell of burnt flesh hovers
on warm summer nights.

When the Quinces Begin to Ripen

"The god of poetry hates those whom fortune smiles upon…
The world is a desert!"
        —Tu Fu

With shaking hand I lift a brush
to compose a letter to my wife. Wondering
whether it will ever reach her. Or even
if she is still alive. A sprig of dogwood
in my belt. A cherished hope.
To see her and my children again…

"Here in a half-barbarous time and country
duckweed grows thick as a man's hand.
Everywhere its deep hue deepens. Standing
at the edge of an endless waste I address
my shadow. Because there is no one else
to converse with. No calling back that wraith
whorled in the wind who haunts this margin
black with storm squall and cloud. Here
the mud stained hem's soon rinsed out.
The broken dyke restored – no crocodile found.
On roadsides the dying, for want of food,
linger. Not for us, or their kind, do the lotuses
in the imperial hot-spring gardens open
punctually each winter. As I look out across
a marsh of fragrant weeds that seems to
go on for ever, I toss a token peck of rice onto
the water in a vain attempt to appease a shadow.

Ten years now and all those years spent wandering.
A thick mist fell like smoke, they said, on
roof-tops and branches the night before
Chang'-an fell. Ominous sounds from all the wells.
Horses in the imperial stables miscarried.
The gatekeepers pawned their virtue many times
that night to a trickle of wealthy merchants.
Money flees before anyone else knows the house
is on fire. And in the inner palaces Yang Guifei
frantic for the syrup of that little god lychee
all the way from the hot south. To assuage
a halitosis compounding beauty. Who dared
place an offering of cherry, blossoming delicate
white cloud, at the ancestral shrine anymore?

A warm south wind gusts now
through the courtyard, shaking the
boughs of the quince tree, as if
it was wrestling with phantoms.
My bones ache. Damp and delirious
I turn over and over without sleeping.
All day the clinking of ice-pedlars
echoed down lane and alley: clear,
hard, cold; as if the mere sound
might allay a fever. The river thrashes
in the gorge beneath the city wall
like an animal tethered for slaughter.
Light goes and fireflies drift in and out
of the screen at the foot of the bed
as if it was a sky woven with portents.

Beneath my window a young man with one arm,
veteran of imperial adventures, pleads for alms.
In thousands of towns and villages far back from
the frontier, he tells a benefactor, nothing
grows but weeds. None are left to recruit, the old
have all flown. On the river miasmal vapours
drift. Last night, like Ming Huang, I dreamed of that
fierce eyed chaser of devils and pestilences Chung K'uei
and his dark dissolving gaze but woke, parched and wet
my forehead still burning, and lay prostrate. Must
I always wake to this: the state's derelictions and
depredations proliferate like wild grass? Outside
in the courtyard a bird sings. The quinces begin to ripen.

This fifth day of fifth moon. People wake early.
The orioles no longer call softly among the willows.
The wisteria blossoms are full. Those who can afford to
buy cakes flavoured with them. All day the poor drift though
the north gate. Cattails and catnips nailed to doors to dispel
plagues, pestilential influences. Today the God is touring
the city, in a tangled procession of images and penitents
scourging their flesh. Inspecting, in his divine excursus,
its health. As if there were an antidote to all the filth
the spirit languishes in, that might purge the source
of the distemper of this imperfect world. I hear them pass
the second sluice, and then cross the river. To
this city of dust I wonder whether they will ever return.

Perhaps there's no cure after all for what assails
us when poets, like birds in winter, flee to the
furthest corners of the earth. The gate-gods, all, are

wearied. No use plastering up their images, mere strips of peeling yellow paper, to ward off calamity when it has already arrived. I roll over and over. My body fire. A dried-up inkstone in a corner, brushes. Almost another life. Yesterday two broken backed mules paused under my window. Their loads a sentence to a short life. And their driver, in rags, sullen, bare footed. There's no escaping. Greed, fear, circumvented compassion. Part, I heard myself repeat from the depth of delirium, of the air we breathe. Then a bird called out. Smell of quince filled the courtyard."

Flowering Midnight

(For Mafruha)

"She was walking like a Greek woman in Hades,
like a Christian woman in Dante's Inferno, carrying
a burden as old as History itself."
                Marguerite Yourcenar

I

Under your collar
starched by the kiss of
flatirons I could smell
a faint scent, like amaretto
or oleander. Mixed
with that of Imperial Leather.

In an arbour, *hortus voluptatis*,
under the dusty boughs
of a linden tree, reclined on
a mossed bank, I imagined
I could hear, as you described
barricades thrown up in haste
at dawn across streets,
dogs bark. "The arbour is full
of noises" you said.

Who heard the bell
that struck the hour
of that midnight feast?

Under your roving hands
fragrant with flowers
there moved, through a grey
twilight, the face of one
I was fated to meet
one drear December
on the outskirts of a city dying
of boredom and fear.

Nails driven or pulled
what was the difference
in that midnight embrace
where solace was not
offered or asked for
and the heart wore
a tattered leaf shadow
a young girl's dress.

In the tedium
of unheated boudoirs
at midnight, cold
and disconsolate,
I counted the hours
waiting for you to arrive,
that sour spittle on your lip
a grape, your leg heavy
as a clod over mine.
A childhood of unassuaged
imaginings wrapped round
your little finger.

In darkness, I began
to suspect, only
did you truly open. Corolla
of empty slogan, cliché, catechism,
lullaby. A closed book:
to the inamorata in the ruined
garden, her vagabond
ghost sucking the dark
bitter pith of its fruit.
In a library of clear water,
a fountain, I saw your
inconsolable expression, heard
you mourning amidst the
apocrypha of each new dawn.

You came, slowly,
to resemble a blind man
stumbling amid ruins
of a past you did not understand.
As if you had dreamed it.
As if the pain of not being
there, in that *locus periucundus*, could
be quenched by tormenting another.
You expected me to dance
amid scattered spolia
to the faded choreography
of an illusion and to sing
to you like a fountain.
A dark ditch, rather,
to irrigate festering roses.

Days spent years later, after you
left on another fundraising and tour,
at the creek head. In a cloud
of mosquitoes, looking at water. Lights
flickered on and off at the shoreline. Then
stayed off: prison and army barracks
exhausting the grid with demands.
Night mingled the cry of victim
and sound of nightingale-thrush.
Over jagged inlet, wetland they floated.
Pain of convulsed limbs, torso
strapped down, merged with acme of
avian ardour. Some listened, offended
disturbed. Most did not.

You were midnight, I realised.
All along. In so many guises, places
and times. In seas of suffocating steerage
and oblivion. In plantations
of immense cruelty. Disavowed.
Your spoor, always changing
always the same. Towards the end
whenever you spoke in that high
pained voice you had perfected over
the years, of pique, irritable
opprobrium, I would hear the rattle
in drawing rooms of glass cabinets
opening. Full of antiques. Smell the stale
pomade of antimacassars eternally
whitening. You were like, I thought,
the old organ grinder on the corner
grinding out, year after year, the same
sad tune. Always, it seemed, at dusk.

On his threadbare clothes, as I passed,
I would smell the same sickly sweet
odour of roses that had never opened.

In a dusk of wood pigeons
and dust caked bowls of silent
fountains of an indebted estate,
on a bed of leaves beneath a tree
full of rotting oranges, they
(gardener and helpmate from
whom the rumour, soon scotched,
entered neighbouring towns)
had come upon you.
In flagrante delicto.
Thrusting, beneath the stained
tearings of a young girl's
dress, and groaning.
Your 'right': to demand
from an indigent's sirings
the youngest and earliest fruit
to spoil, in lui of confiscation
of all he possessed. For which
no doubt later you would return:
your kind never getting enough.

II

Bright spurge and amaryllis.
A fragrant surrogate, an *arbor
Paradisi*, runs through all our days.
And like love, an old love, is, O
an old sore. Worked up,
under the collar, into
a poisonous malaise, it spreads.

Whored to prosperity, a bankrupt
pastoral: to the dictatorship of the rich.

III

I remembered days when he'd come back
smelling like a bunch of sweet grass:
dust of road, culm, attached
to him. Hand sweat tasting of
leather. Oil and unguent could erase
palm scars scored by reins. Redress
ravages of wind, sun. Too deep, though,
for them to erase, that shadow
midnight drew through my life. And draws
through the life of each of us and which,
like fallen angels, we can neither flee nor
acknowledge. Too deep for them, too,
to erase, that sound of dogs
tearing flesh in the scented arbour.
Delivered to them each day
until they'd developed a taste for it.
Staked out for them. Still talking:
while musicians played and ladies
under parasols, sipping cool
cordials, chattered and applauded.

He was my *daemon meridianus*
coming to lie with me,
"spell-stopp'd",
under the linden tree
in the cool breeze
bearing the scent of flowers

and incense. A dark breath-
ed censer dispensing endearments
into my heart. Bondage. Not bower.

And he was my north
ima praecipitari
turned into my south.
Wherever I turned to look
midnight masqueraded as dawn.
My true alignment became north.
So much so that night
deepened and whitened about me
removing 'impurities', 'stains'. All
opposites dissolved. A winnowing
of voices. Only his,
white cantor, dark tongue,
could be heard.

Under his collar,
halter, greasy white noose,
I inserted, at last, thumbs
and fingers and pulled. Tight. Till
those words liberté, égalité, fraternité,
sepulchres for bleeding ghosts,
choked in his throat. Saying:
"Broken philosophe, apothecary
no poultice, no potion, no salve
for the wound? Try this
garrot slowly turned, by one
of those with two legs
your kind first herded, penned."

From Tide Washed Salterns

"So sweet a smell … as if we had bene
in the midst of some delicate garden."
      Arthur Barlowe, *The Roanoke Voyages 1584–1590*

On salt eaten quays
beside dark copses of alders
in the midday heat of a false
summer, who will deliver them
from their transgressions
their restless stratagems and
narrow tyrannies: latter day heroes
mouthing cruel platitudes of their
congeners. From the submerged
chapel at the shoreline, from
the miry track from the ferry
leading northward, pilgrims
with their pyxides of holy water,
loud-talking, they went
seeking the ideal city
"lusting for it like pigs" to far
off isles, dispensing terror,
signing their names
in the black smoke of ruins,
not looking back – to tide washed, wild
flower salterns littered with
cracked brine pans where barges
were hovelled wharfwards, to
angled bastions of old Dutch
embankments where first Spring
droughts baked the creeks' ditch
hollows and driftways
iron hard, to quiet deliberations
by which they were found wanting.

When they returned they moved
amongst us as if nothing had happened
out of the ordinary course of events
displaying mementoes of far places
brass fingerbowls, flagons, ceremonial
scabbards, buffed and buffed
until they glowed in dark sculleries,
on staircases. Who, now, will
redeem them: from their violent
intolerance and ways? From
salt fretted wastes they troop still
down the centuries. Like ghosts
returning to roost they enter
our streets and houses,
propounding old platitudes
refurbished but the same.
In the smoking ruins
of a dream endlessly intoning
them, old men with a hard
intemperate gaze, they wait.
Sea asters droop now
beside derelict quays
at the creek heads
in the first Spring droughts.
Out of the cracked earth
an exhausted incubus rises.

The Carved Serpent

"Oh flowering futility of the world…"
    Tasos Leivaditis *The Scent of the Night*

Snow falls. Moment
by moment. Carpeting
the black thorn porch
of a church, serpent coiled
but repulsed, and a higgledy
piggledy main street
working its way up from
the marsh. A dark music
fills the air. In a ploughed
field a battered cuirass
buried for centuries
begins to emerge. A bird sings
in the alder trees beside
the road. Nightlong it sings.

You lie awake.
Listening for the sound
of a thaw. Roads
impassable. Wind. History
is a dark field ploughed
again and again,
harvest we cannot atone
for. Ghost acreages
tilled by invisible hands.
And this snow, falling
and falling.

In a dream you stumble
through deep drifts.
From farmstead

to ruined farmstead.
A broken compass
in your hand. *In how many
guises do you appear
before us, make yourself
known to us?* All the embankments
eroded. The churchyard
a bare mound. No footprint
but the wind's. And
the chimeras, *We were
slothful and
inattentive ... Who, now,
should we accuse if
not ourseleves?*, are
gathering again in the
black thorn porch.
In an alder tree
beside the road
a bird is singing.

Night

"I have come to lead you to the other shore;
into eternal darkness, into fire and into ice."
         Dante *Inferno*: [III: 86-87]

Faint mist over the salt marsh.
Broken-up horizon. Jib and boom.
Wharves given over to trinkets.
Roadways full of those
with an entranced gaze
heading off into the future.
At frostbitten terminals
and quays they breathe, in a city
in whose overgrown parks and weed-
locked sidings the homeless
each night lay their heads,
a twilight of contaminated moments

Like light, disinterring at end
of day each rufous tint
entombed in sandstone wall,
night collects you. Fragment
upon uneasy fragment. Collects
what can't be counted or
observed beyond the act of counting
and collating. What is forged
in a moment of surrender, after
the moment has extinguished itself.

Evening. Warm with a wind
of tar and oil off
the river. In a ruined garden
under willow and aspen
afloat on the debris of all
lived moments, fireflies rise
and fall, ignite and die
in the scented dusk
beneath the trees. You stand,
for a while, watching
the slow interstitial ebb
and flow of their light.
Moment by moment. Adrift
on the current of fire that
moves through everything. That
everything moves toward
in a moment of surrender.

Forsaken, primordial moment.
No returning to where the path
was lost on an afternoon you have
forgotten. Overcast and shrouded
in drizzle. Caught between two states
comprehending, fully, neither.

On the cold stones of an ambrosial
coast, having sacrificed nothing
and given up everything,
they place their feet. Over the salt marsh,
burying that "old mongrel world"
of latchgate and driftway

that pre-technoparadiso,
the snow lies deep. Lights
on quay and terminal,
through thickly falling flakes,
flash. On. Off. On. Off. Like
fireflies under blossoming trees.

At the time before mind
asserted itself over the tumult
of all successive moments:
weaving a pattern, keeping
it alive in that continuous
thread of overlapping instants
parting, re-joining. Knitting
them up. When sitting alone at
the window. When scent of phlox
from the garden entered the room.
When you neither heard what
was said, nor appeared to listen
your mind alert only to that
unrecovered moment into which
history had not inserted itself.

On the unkempt corner of a street, time of edicts
and false proclamations, the future breaks
against them: in sabotaged out-of-work towns
of blackened brickwork. In small stores boarded up,
bankrupted lives. The bookshops all gone.
Word-hoard held in a cloud. No longer burned
but, like memory, deleted. As they stand there
"material for an inhuman experiment", snow falls

*again on everything. The frozen kerbside.
Yesterday. Tomorrow. Great blank, the coldest
and whitest of all incunabulas, descending
on time's fevered formations, insignia. And no port any
longer for them to turn to, outrunning the storm.*

And the pattern, that
an instant shatters and
repairs, becomes an end
in itself. And the path,
on an afternoon you have
forgotten, can't be restored.
Imposed upon each
living moment, woven in
the flesh: a pattern. Settling
on inlet and embankment
in a twilight of mist and rain.
Until you, conjured from
the debris of all lived
moments, cannot tell where
it and you begin, end.

Nostos

Always it is the same. History
is a handful of tired pieties, predilections:
animosities of attachment of grasper
and grasped. Affirming a transitory
and tenuous existence, the plenitude
of a present which cannot last. And
its last moment is also its first
in an infinite series of moments renewed.

The diffused aromas of a lost
summer hover around a faded grey
gatepost in a field. Discarded
fragments of a life surrendered.
One to come: beyond this moment,
hesitant, but sure. One, the spider
spinning in the wainscot a new
death and a beginning for us, we are
reluctant, mired in the immense nostalgia
for all lost moments, to forgo.

* * *

"In my hours of gloom ... what is left for me but to seek out the true, lost face of music somewhere off in the forest ... among the birds."

Olivier Messiaen

[From Preface to score of *Quartet for the End of Time* composed and first performed in Stalag 8-A, 1941]

* * *

Notes

Epigraph
Nightingales: as of 2018 their numbers had diminished in the UK, along with numerous other bird species, by over 90%.

Dedication
An English Master who in the words of Horace *"carminis nomenque dedit poetae"*: you have conferred on me the name of poet. His friend, the poet Martin Bell, penned for him this memorable quatrain:

> *Prospect 1939 (For Campbell Matthews)*
>
> 'Life is a journey' said our education.
> And so we packed, although we found it slow.
> At twenty one, left stranded at the station,
> We've heaps of luggage and nowhere to go.

Rock Star Celebrates Birthday at Exclusive Country House Retreat

Quotation in the text: from Ben Jonson, *To Penshurst*

Road to the North

FIRE: acronym for the Finance, Insurance and Real Estate sector which accounts for most increases in wealth in modern western capitalism.

House of Finance: the Mithraic remains are preserved in London in the basement of the headquarters of the American financial-data giant Bloomberg.

Turnpikes: Henry VII's 1489 act 'Agaynst the Pulling Doun of Touns'.

Quotations in the text in order: UK National Archives (re: Kenya) Kew; Sir Charles Noble Arden-Clarke (Gold Coast); *Epic of Gilgamesh*; Isaac Walton.

Alder

In Lapp the word 'lei'be' denoting the alder tree also denotes menstrual blood and bear's blood, constituting an etymological site where pre-Neolithic, and early Neolithic, beliefs are preserved.

Where No Snow Falls

Quotation in the text: from the *Odyssey* ... According to classicist Rhys Carpenter, Salmoxis, a Thracian god of immortality and said to have worn a bear skin, provided the thematic material, of prolonged disappearance and sudden reappearance, for the poem composed during a period of early Greek mercantilist expansion in the Mediterranean. The kind of immortality which Salmoxis represented, however, was not the "deathless immortality" of the Olympians (or lesser state of rejuvenescence which Athena bestows upon that returned and ageing Hero who the poet George Seferis characterised as a man "of inconstancy, of wanderings and of wars") but the older palingenesis of life, death and new life which the disappearing and reappearing bear, as master of renewal and the wheel of seasons, emerging just ahead of the snow melt with her young, appeared to embody. Telemachus, son of Odysseus, refers to his grandfather as Arkeisius, "bear son", the result of Cephalus mating with a she-bear, confirming the ancient matrilineal and pre-Indo-European myth of a line founded by bear-human marriage.

Reliquary

Quotation in the text: from the Buddhist logician Nagarjuna.

Road of Dust

The road of the title refers to that leading to Kaifeng where Li Yu, poet, musician, painter, devout Buddhist and last emperor of the Southern Tsang Dynasty, was transported after Taizu's army's protracted investiture of his capital city Nanjing (Jinling) which, in the winter of 976 CE, finally fell. For years Taizu, emperor of the subsequent Sung Dynasty, had conducted an aggressive military policy of intimidation, destabilisation and invasion of independent minded states in an attempt to bring all of them and their resources under his control. The Southern Tang state was the last to succumb.

In Chinese Buddhism dust refers to the realms of the six senses, consciousness regarded as one of them. Hence 'dust-consciousness'. Such consciousness, likened to the bustle and sensory allure of a marketplace, is seen to obscure the underlying nature of perception.

Quotation in the text: from the Buddhist logician Nagarjuna.

Under Jiu-yi Shan

Regarded as the 'father' of Chinese poetry and whose foundational poem *Li Sao* struck a clear political note of dissent: "Let us be clear: it is hopeless! The state has no statesman." Ch'u Yuan was a leading minister in the State of Chu (the same state in which during the Warring States period Lao Tzu author of the *Tao Teh Ching* was born) during the fourth and third century BCE; a time, like today, of remorseless wars. Because of court rivalries, "Day and night they curse and vilify me", and of his hostility to the growing power of the State of Chin, a Legalist highly centralised and authoritarian state (similar to, in the West, Justinian's Christian state) which would give its name to the region we now identify as China, he was exiled south to a non-Sinitic culture and region, present day Hunan, where he traversed ceaselessly the vast undrained swamps and wetlands around the Dongting lakes: "I weep for sweet herbs among foul weeds ... With trembling heart I wander the marshlands." His famous long poem *Li Sao* (Encountering Sorrow) was profoundly influenced by the shamanistic songs and lore of the region. His death by his own hand in the Miluo River is commemorated, each fifth day of the fifth month of the traditional lunisolar calendar, by the dragon boat festival. The dragon on the boat prow is a motif which derives from the crocodile. *Under Jiu-yi Shan* (Nine Doubt Mountain, a site in southern Hunan sacred as the burial place of Shun one of the most revered rulers of antiquity noted for his moral stature) embeds various lines from *Li Sao* and observations on Ch'u Yuan by Su-ma Ch'ien the Great Recorder of the first century BCE.

A Country Without Names

Quotations in the text in order: Thomas Jefferson, Edward Gibbon, George Seferis.

When the Quinces Begin to Ripen

Tu Fu was a very minor official in the Chinese capital Chang'-an in the northern part of the country. A rebellion by An Lu-shan in 755 captured the capital and very nearly ended the Tsang dynasty. Tu Fu, who was not there at the time, was taken prisoner by the rebels and taken to Chang'-an. He eventually escaped and joined the imperial court and was rewarded with a higher position on its return to Chang'-an. But he was far too outspoken, especially on issues of social justice, for his own good and was, fortunately, only demoted. He was posted to a minor position in an out of the way location. It was perhaps during this time, or sometime later, he contracted malaria. Eventually, after many enforced wanderings over what had become an unstable country where the rebellion spawned many other rebellions for many years, he retired and in 766 arrived and lived the last years of his life in K'uei-chou in the far southern region of Hunan where the poet Ch'u Yuan ("that wraith") had, many centuries before, been exiled. He stayed there for two years, bitterly lamenting his "failure in a ruined Empire". Attempting to set off north again for his birthplace with, finally, his family, perhaps in response to another rebellion brewing nearby, he died whilst still in Hunan.

Emperor Ming-huang (712–756), suffering from a fever, went to sleep and in a dream was tormented by a demon. Suddenly the imposing figure of Chung K'uei appeared in his dream and killed the demon. On waking the emperor's fever had gone and he subsequently canonised Chung K'uei as: "Great Spiritual Chaser of Demons for the Whole Empire".

Yang Guifei was the young wife of the Emperor Ming-huang.

[Some degree of sentiment regarding use of Chinese names employing the Wade-Giles system of Romanisation has led, in the 'Chinese' poems and the Notes, to inconsistencies. Having for almost half a century lived

115

with, for instance, Tu Fu as phonologically just that I have not wished to jettison it for the now more generally used Du Fu. Other names, using the official Pin-yin system, having come upon them only relatively recently, I have had no such qualms about. The original Wade-Giles forms, however, in which some names first presented themselves to me all those years ago, have been retained.]

From Tide Washed Salterns

Quotation in the text: from Bernardino de Sahagún, *The Florentine Codex*

Night

Quotations in the text in order: Alexander Blok, *The Twelve*; Maxim Gorky, *The New Life*.

www.ingramcontent.com/pod-product-compliance
Lightning Source LLC
Chambersburg PA
CBHW031404160426
43196CB00007B/886